OUR BUNDLE OF JOY

Thoughts to Celebrate a New Life

Selected by Bruce Lansky

Meadowbrook Press

Distributed by Simon & Schuster
New York

Library of Congress Cataloging-in-Publication Data
Our bundle of joy : thoughts to celebrate a new life / selected by Bruce Lansky.
    p. cm.
    ISBN 0-88166-391-3 (Meadowbrook) ISBN 0-743-21618-0 (Simon & Schuster)
    1. Infants—Poetry. 2. Infants—Quotations, maxims, etc. I. Lansky, Bruce.

PN6110.I52 O95 2001
808.81'93520542—dc21

2001032604

Editorial Director: Christine Zuchora-Walske
Coordinating Editor and Copyeditor: Joseph Gredler
Proofreader: Megan McGinnis
Production Manager: Paul Woods
Desktop Publishing: Danielle White
Cover Photo: Dia Max/FPG Int.

© 2001 by Meadowbrook Creations

Published by Meadowbrook Press, 5451 Smetana Drive, Minnetonka, Minnesota 55343

www.meadowbrookpress.com

BOOK TRADE DISTRIBUTION by Simon & Schuster, a division of Simon and Schuster, Inc., 1230 Avenue of the Americas, New York, New York 10020

05 04 03 02 01   10 9 8 7 6 5 4 3 2 1

Printed in Italy

Dedication

To Sienna, my first granddaughter.
When your father was a baby, I loved him
as much as he now loves you.

Acknowledgments

We would like to thank the photographers who contributed to this book:

p. vi © Rob Lewine/Corbis Stock Market; p. 7 © www.comstock.com; p. 12 © Paul Kuroda/SuperStock; p. 17 © Florian Franke/SuperStock; p. 20 © Kathy Collins/FPG Int.; p. 25 © Mel Yates/FPG Int.; p. 32 © Michele-Salmieri/FPG Int.; p. 41 © Michael Segal/SuperStock; p. 44 © Bavaria Bildagentur/FPG Int.; p. 49 © Anna Lundgren/SuperStock; p. 54 © Marylin Nolt; p. 59 © Michele-Salmieri/FPG Int.; p. 62 © www.comstock.com; p. 69 © Barbara Peacock/FPG Int.; p. 74 © Robert Kaufman; p. 79 © Stephen Simpson/FPG Int.; p. 84 © Craig Hammell/Corbis Stock Market

We also wish to thank the individuals who served on reading panels for this project:

Sharon Hart Addy, Margerie Goggin Allen, Sylvia Andrews, Joan Marie Arbogast, Ken Bastien, Shirley Bingham, Sonja Brown, Anita Gevauden Byerly, Maureen Cannon, Gail Clark, Faye Click, Eileen Daily, Holly Davis, Rebecca Kai Dotlich, Samantha Dunaway, Julia Nunnally Duncan, S. M. Eichner, Gene Fehler, Connie Jordan Green, Ellen Jackson, Judi James, Kim Koehler, Billie Marsh, Barbara J. Mayer, Barbara Merchant, Gail Minthorn, Lois Muehl, Lorraine Bates Noyes, Lawrence Schimel, Rosemary Schmidt, Mary Scott, Jacqueline Seewald, Sherry Waas Shunfenthal, Nancy Sweetland, Denise Ann Tiffany, Maren Tirabessi, Esther Towns, Debra Tracy, Evelyn Amuedo Wade, Toni Webb, Jory Westberry, Vicki Wiita

Contents

THE ANSWER OF LOVE

We see it in
each other's eyes
every time our
daydreams touch.
That other part of us
that's still to come,
that promise
that holds us
even when we sleep,
that little
answer of love
that soon will
fill the cradle
that now only rocks
in the corner
of our eyes.

Charles Ghigna

DANCING BABY

I felt you dance into me.
Oh, some babies are born
of hot, wide passion;
others in a cool, momentary
indifference with untroubled sleep the
real reward.

But you danced in
with the moon waxed and
your daddy singing a love song
to the sky,

a song with my name and
yours ribboning through it
until there was a chain so
long, so strong, that
you had no choice but to
follow it, to join our joy,
to dance into my belly and
rest untroubled for
nine lovely months until you
were ready to sing your own
love song.

Laurie Lico Albanese

Fortunately, I changed, without realizing it at first. Soon everyone around me began to exclaim how well I looked and how cheerful I was. The half-hidden and involuntary smile of pregnant women showed even through my makeup.

Colette

Annabelle felt in love with the world. She wanted to touch the grass, the trees, the sky, hug the air. She was part of everything and everything was one great big miracle. Sometimes she wanted to call her mother and ask, "Is this the way you felt when you carried me?"

Ruth Moose

"Her condition" was her own choice, and she'd waited a long time for it. She was enjoying it…most of the time. She didn't enjoy the twinges in her back, nor feeling like Humpty Dumpty, not being able to see her toes…but she did like feeling for the first time that her body could do wonderful things, that she was a special person doing something only she could do.

Ruth Moose

There are two things in this life for which we are never fully prepared and that is—twins.

Josh Billings

A friend of a friend looked at my stomach and said, "Don't rush; it's the best baby-sitter you'll ever have."

Karen Scott Boates

With fewer than twenty weeks to go, I was slowly realizing that the finely tuned life David and I had evolved together was on the verge of extinction.

Roberta Israeloff

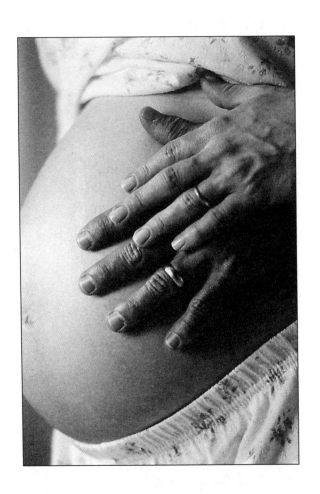

DADDY LOVES YOU

Hello busy-little-baby-
in-your-mother's-belly-
with-no-name-yet.
Can you hear me?
This is your daddy speaking.
It's two in the morning.
All your kicking and fussing
is keeping your mother awake.
And her tossing and turning
is keeping me awake.
So close your eyes
and try to catch some z's.
That's right, it's sleepy time…
time for beddy-bye.
Lullaby…go to sleep…
da da daa daa da daa da.
That's a good little boy or girl…
you'll feel a lot better
with a good night's sleep.
(And so will we.)
Sweet dreams.
Daddy loves you.

Bruce Lansky

A recent story tells about a baby who was giggling and laughing minutes after he was born. The obstetrician noticed he had unusual muscle control, his tiny fist being tightly clenched. When the doctor pried it open, he found a contraceptive pill.

Evan Esar

If all is dim and quiet, warm and peaceful, the baby will relax after his traumatic journey. His breathing will steady. His crumpled face will smooth itself out and his eyes will open. His head will lift a little and his limbs will move against your skin. Put very gently to your bare breast, he may suck, discover a new form of human contact and feel a little less separated. These are his first moments with his new world: let him make them without distress. These are his first moments of life; let him have them in peace.

Penelope Leach

The moment a child is born,
the mother is also born.
She never existed before.
The woman existed, but the mother, never.
A mother is something absolutely new.

Rajneesh

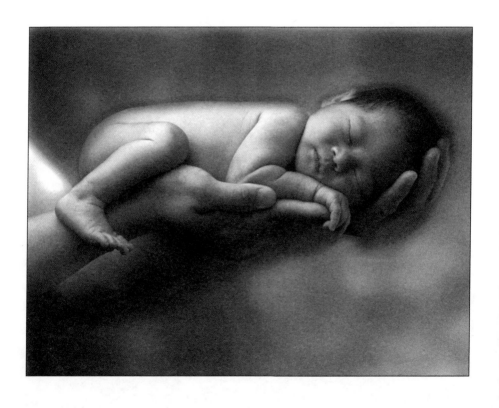

TO THE NEWBORN (EXCERPT)

Like a round loaf, that's how small you were.
I rolled you on the board with my palm,
I kneaded you, patted you,
greased you smooth, floured you,
I shaped your roly body.
You slept in the palm of my hands.
You'd hardly dawned, your slight bones
were still soft under your skin, yet
how vehemently your vulnerable life
pulsed in your tiny torso, your folded limbs
closed about you like thick petals,
beneath, you slept like the still of a rose.

Judit Toth

MORNING SONG

Love set you going like a fat gold watch.
The midwife slapped your footsoles, and your bald cry
Took its place among the elements.

Our voices echo, magnifying your arrival. New statue.
In a drafty museum, your nakedness
Shadows our safety. We stand round blankly as walls.

I'm no more your mother
Than the cloud that distills a mirror to reflect its own slow
Effacement at the wind's hand.

All night your moth-breath
Flickers among the flat pink roses. I wake to listen:
A far sea moves in my ear.

One cry, and I stumble from bed, cow-heavy and floral
In my Victorian nightgown.
Your mouth opens clean as a cat's. The window square

Whitens and swallows its dull stars. And now you try
Your handful of notes;
The clear vowels rise like balloons.

Sylvia Plath

NEWBORN

Big-headed
in a knitted cap,

cocooned in flannel
strewn with yellow bunnies,

tiny fingers curl into
Lilliputian fists and

cuff the talcum-scented air as
he roars for Mom

who is lush with love and
sustenance.

Irene Sedeora

To a Newborn

My own little Buddha—
we don't speak the same language yet,
but your wisdom shines through your eyes.

Betsy Franco

There came to port last Sunday night
    The queerest little craft,
Without an inch of rigging on;
    I looked and looked—and laughed.
It seemed so curious that she
    Should cross the unknown water,
And moor herself within my room—
    My daughter! O my daughter!

G. W. Cable

NEWBORN

Soft as a warm bun,
you rise in your basket:
your yeasty breath,
sweet as morning;
your face, a road map
about to be traveled;
your eyes, clean as rain;
nothing on this earth is quite so new.

Barbara Crooker

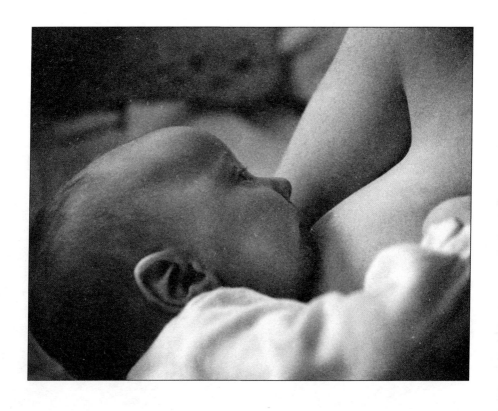

A little child born yesterday,
A thing on mother's milk and kisses fed.

Homer

A soft cheek nestled close to mine. Warm breaths in an easy rhythm. The fragrant aroma of my sweet baby. My arms engulf her. I never want to let go.

Sherri Waas Shunfenthal

You feel so much love for your child that you wonder how you could possibly love the second one as much. Then you discover how infinite your capacity to love is.

Linda D'Agrosa

Our first child helps us to discover the depth of love; our second child, the breadth of it.

Beth Wilson Saavedra

My child looked at me and I looked back at him in the delivery room, and I realized that out of a sea of infinite possibilities it had come down to this: a specific person, born on the hottest day of the year, conceived on Christmas Eve, made by his father and me miraculously from scratch.

Anna Quindlen

Leave it to a baby to turn your world upside down, take your breath away, and make you fall in love again. With his toothless grin, your baby sets your heart on fire.

Jan Blaustone

23

If I hadn't had a child, I'd never have known that most elemental, direct, true relationship. I don't know if I'd fully understand the values of society that I prize. I would have missed some of the mystery of life and death. Not to know how a child grows, the wonder of a newborn's hand . . . . I have been fortunate.

Diane Feinstein

During the first weeks, I used to lie long hours with the baby in my arms, watching her asleep; sometimes catching a gaze from her eyes; feeling very near the edge, the mystery, perhaps the knowledge of Life . . .

Isadora Duncan

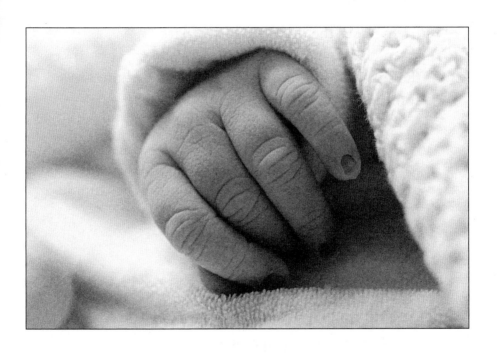

THE ADOPTION

I remember the quiet room, the dark
green chair where we sat afternoons,
the sun—no matter how tightly shuttered out—
coming in and curving across us
as if we were not separate, but a single body
joined in a ceremony of light.
My legs beneath you, my arms around you,
my breast under the glass bottle with rubber nipple,
I talked to you and sang to you.
No one interrupted us.
The dog sat quietly in the corner.
If I could have given birth to you,
I would have. I would have taken you
inside me, held you
and given birth to you again.

All the hours we spent in that room. Then,
one day, with your eyes focused on mine, you
reached up and stroked my cheek. Your touch
was that of the inchworm on its aerial thread
just resting on my skin, a larval curve
alighting and lifting off, a lightness
practicing for the time it will have wings.

I like to think wherever you go, you will
keep some memory of sunlight in the room
where I first loved you, and you first loved.

Fran Castan

MOTHERS

Oh mother,
here in your lap,
as good as a bowlful of clouds,
I your greedy child
am given your breast,
the sea wrapped in skin,
and your arms,
roots covered with moss
and with new shoots sticking out
to tickle the laugh out of me.
Yes, I am wedded to my teddy
but he has the smell of you
as well as the smell of me.
Your necklace that I finger
is all angel eyes.

Your rings that sparkle
are like the moon on the pond.
Your legs that bounce me up and down,
your dear nylon-covered legs,
are the horses I will ride
into eternity.

Oh mother,
after this lap of childhood
I will never go forth
into the big people's world
as an alien,
a fabrication,
or falter
when someone else
is as empty as a shoe.

Anne Sexton

PERSPECTIVE

Lying on our backs,
my baby and I
watch the fall leaves
fly through the air:
like gold finches,
they swoop and glide.
Trees meet above us
in turrets and towers;
a mobile of branches
catches the light;
a kaleidoscope of color
has fallen around us;
we are showered in gold,
coined and minted.

Looking through your eyes
I see
a carousel world
of magic and light.

Barbara Crooker

PRECIOUS CHILD

Diamonds sparkle in your eyes
as grins of gleaming pearls arise
and sterling silver songs unfold
through ruby lips, from heart of gold.
Oh, precious child, until your birth
I didn't know what life was worth.

Sydnie Meltzer Kleinhenz

In the sheltered simplicity of the first days after a baby is born, one sees again the magical closed circle, the miraculous sense of two people existing only for each other, the tranquil sky reflected on the face of the mother nursing her child.

Anne Morrow Lindbergh

I saw his eyes open full to mine, and realized each of us was fastened to the other, not only by mouth and breast, but through our mutual gaze: the depth, calm, passion, of that dark blue, maturely focused look.

Adrienne Rich

ADOPTION

I stitched us together by night
in the rocking chair, marveled
at your fingers, the foreign navel,
memorized the sweep of your eyebrows,
unraveled your language.
Having accepted the unfamiliar,
I kept watch
for proof of our union.

Tonight I inhale as I kiss
your perfect face, moist
from busy dreaming. Your fragrance
marks me—that fingerprint
only a parent can read.
I crawl in beside you, grateful
and patient, to dip us
with even breath
in this night's ink.

Alison Kolodinsky

THREE WOMEN: A POEM FOR THREE VOICES (EXCERPT)

What did my fingers do before they held him?
What did my heart do, with its love?
I have never seen a thing so clear.
His lids are like the lilac-flower
And soft as a moth, his breath.
I shall not let go.

Sylvia Plath

BREATHE DEEP

Whole-wheat bread
baking a crisp crust
on a December morning,

fresh-mown bluegrass
under the July sun,

hamburgers grilling
over a charcoal fire,

red clover
blooming
in a Kansas field,

apple muffins
split and steaming cinnamon
as the butter melts,

a Peace rose
in a crystal bowl
on my kitchen table;

my baby boy,
bathed and powdered,
cuddling against my cheek.

Life is full.
Just breathe
deep.

Sheryl Nelms

THE MOTHER'S SONG

My little boy is sleeping on the ledge.
On his back he lies, breathing through his open mouth,
his little stomach is bulging round—
is it strange if I start to cry with joy?

Eskimo

MOVED

I move her,
baking in sunlight, into my shade.
Sleeping, she suckles an invisible breast
as if I were still attached,
still full of the sweetness
that fattened those cheeks, those thighs,
that flesh like kneaded dough, rising.
I marvel at her plumpness,
at myself for filling her so fully
with nothing more, no others needed;
I feed on *her* now.
She yawns, and as her eyes open,
she spoons a smile into my hungry heart
where it warms me like no oven.

Margaret Park Bridges

SIMON

heartcake   heartcake
    sweetened with breastmilk
    rising with kisses
the whole house warmed
by the fragrance
           of your smile

Susan Eisenberg

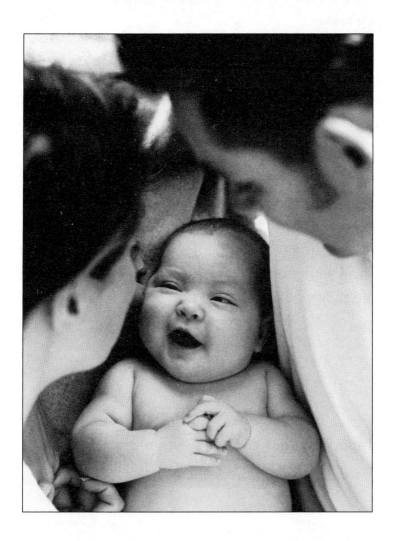

When you're drawing up your list of life's miracles, you might place near the top the first moment your baby smiles at you.

Bob Greene

It's an interesting fact that babies who won't smile for love or money will smile for vegetables. And the messier the vegetable the more they will smile.

Jean Kerr

There's this moment when your baby cries and you pick her up and suddenly she's all smiles—it's magic.

Hope Steadman (from thirtysomething*)*

No flower is as fragrant as a baby after a bath.

Sherri Waas Shunfenthal

How delicate the skin, how sweet the breath of children!

Euripides

The child was brought in, its infant beauty shining like a jewel in the grayness of the dawn.

Murasaki Shikibu

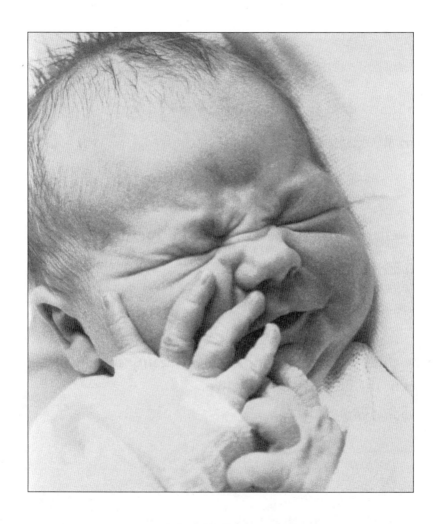

MINIATURE

My day-old son is plenty scrawny,
His mouth is wide with screams, or yawny,
His ears seem larger than he's needing.
His nose is flat, his chin receding,
His skin is very, very red,
He has no hair upon his head,
And yet I'm proud as proud can be
To hear you say he looks like me.

Richard Armour

His mother's eyes,
His father's chin,
His auntie's nose,
His uncle's grin,

His great-aunt's hair,
His grandma's ears,
His grandpa's mouth,
So it appears...

Poor little tot,
Well may he moan.
He hasn't much
To call his own.

Richard Armour

ON WATCHING YOUR FRIEND TRYING TO MAKE HER BABY DRINK FROM A CUP FOR THE FIRST TIME

Sip a little
Sup a little
From your little
Cup a little
Sup a little
Sip a little
Put it to your
Lip a little
Tip a little
Tap a little
Not into your
Lap or it'll
Drip a little
Drop a little
On the table
Top a little!

James Kirkup

THE ANATOMY OF MELANCHOLY

A little baby, when she cries,
Is a spectacular surprise.

Assorted lines distort her face,
And of her eyes there's not a trace.

Her infant nose has vanished, too,
And left a button for a clue.

But most mysterious of all,
Her rosebud mouth, which was so small,

Has suddenly become, instead,
A good deal bigger than her head.

Margaret Fishback

THE BABY

The cat
who purrs
so sweetly
cannot fathom
why her place
in our bed
has been taken
by this one
who cries.

Susan Eisenberg

The first cry of a newborn baby in Chicago or Zamboango, in Amsterdam or Rangoon, has the same pitch and key, each saying, "I am! I have come through! I belong! I am a member of the Family!"

Carl Sandburg

I stood in the hospital corridor the night after she was born. Through a window I could see all the small, crying newborn infants, and somewhere among them slept the one who was mine. I stood there for hours filled with happiness until the night nurse sent me to bed.

Liv Ullman

FOR MOLLY (A VERBAL CUDDLE FOR AN EIGHT-MONTH-OLD)

You—the purest pleasure
of my life,
the split pit
that proves
the ripeness of the fruit,
the unbroken center
of my broken hopes—

O little one,
making you
has centered my lopsided life

so that if I know
a happiness
that reason never taught,
it is because of your small
unreasonably wrigglish
limbs.
Daughter, little bean,
sprout, sproutlet, smallest
girleen,
just saying your name
makes me grin.

I used to hate the word Mother,
found it obscene,
& now I love it
since that is me
to you.

Erica Jong

I actually remember feeling delight, at two o'clock in the morning, when the baby woke for his feed, because I so longed to have another look at him.

Margaret Drabble

Who is getting the most pleasure from this rocking, the baby or me?

Nancy Thayer

While doting on our newborn, I realized how much my parents must have doted on me.

Bruce Lansky

FIRSTBORN

Who in that warm
And watery dark
Seemed no more
Than a question mark

Bursts wide the door
And with a cry
Affirms she is
Triumphant I.

Charles W. Pratt

Whenver we take a trip, we have to enlist the help of thirteen sherpas, a chaffeur, two maids, and a nanny—and that's only for the baby's luggage.

Ginger Hinchman

The baby has learned to know and love you better than anyone else and now he wants you all the time and all to himself…. His ideal would be your continual presence and constant attention.

Penelope Leach

My baby cries—and all the world is wrong.
My baby laughs—the world is full of song.

Hindustanic proverb

He is at the height of his powers. If he closes his eyes, he causes the world to disappear. If he opens his eyes, he causes the world to come back. If there is harmony within him, the world is harmonious. If rage shatters his inner harmony, the unity of the world is shattered. If desire arises within him, he utters the magic syllables that cause the desired object to appear. His wishes, his thoughts, his gestures, his noises command the universe.

Selma H. Fraiberg

People who say they sleep like a baby usually don't have one.

Leo J. Burke

Sometimes you think you can barely take care of yourself, and yet here you are holding your new baby. Someone up there must believe in you.

Jan Blaustone

There are times when parenthood seems like nothing but feeding the mouth that bites you.

Peter De Vries

There are only two lasting bequests we can hope to give our children. One of these is roots, the other wings.

Hodding Carter

When we had our first baby, we could hardly believe he belonged to us. Once he was grown, it took him years to convince us he didn't.

Susan D. Anderson

What a pleasure it used to be to go to the bathroom alone.

Bruce Lansky

I had heard about the negatives—the fatigue, the loneliness, the loss of self. But nobody told me about the wonderful parts: holding my baby close to me, seeing her first smile, watching her grow and become more responsive day by day…. For the first time, I cared about somebody else more than myself, and I would do anything to nurture and protect her.

from The New Our Bodies, Ourselves

You don't want to leave home in the morning and you can't wait to get home at night. She's changing all the time.

John Goodman

TWENTY-FIVE YEARS LATER

Looking back on that day,
I remember that I didn't love you
immediately and without reservation,
the way books said I should.

How was I to love someone I didn't
know how to feed? And what if
the bath water was too hot,
or I didn't sing to you enough?

Curiosity followed abject fear,
and then a quiet sort of liking.
As for love, it padded in like the old cat
who purred himself into your crib.

I wonder…
do you remember those
first tentative touches,
those nights I cried with you?

Perhaps it is good if you do.
Maybe we need that tempering
to remind us how empty life was
before love filled our two hearts.

Karen Hammond

HAVING GIVEN BIRTH

for the first time,

my body comes back
to itself.

Stretch marks on my breasts
fade pale
as milk.

Around my head, songs
from my childhood quiver
like moths. They ask
to be taken back,
they ask forgiveness
for having been gone so long.

Through my own lips,
my mother's voice
sings my daughter to sleep.

When she sleeps
at my breast, I become
the oldest person
I have ever known.

I am younger than I can remember.

Ingrid Wendt

Tell me, what is half so sweet
As a baby's tiny feet?

Edgar A. Guest

PRAYER FOR A NEW MOTHER (EXCERPT)

Let her have laughter with her little one;
    Teach her the endless, tuneless songs to sing,
Grant her the right to whisper to her son
    The foolish names one dare not call a king.

Dorothy Parker

STARRY EYED

Our baby stares up at the mobile
We have just installed.
A lemon-yellow sun,
A purple moon,
Different colored stars,
Turning gently, this way and that.
All held in heaven by pretty strings.
Our daughter's unblinking eyes,
Wide with wonder.
Discovering the universe
For the very first time.

Robert Scotellaro

The world he discovers is a vast and intricate jig-saw puzzle, thousands of pieces scrambled together in a crazy juxtaposition, piece by piece he assembles the fragments into whole objects and the objects into groups until he emerges with a fairly coherent picture of the tiny piece of world he inhabits…. This learning…is a prodigious intellectual feat. No wonder every parent thinks his baby is a genius. He is!

Selma H. Fraiberg

I placed Ben's head on my knees, his body stretched out along my thighs, and lifted his head to mine, taking a quick catch breath before saying "Benjamin" and dropping him back down. After a few rounds he stared into my eyes, waiting for me to begin again. He had caught on. A synapse in his brain hooked up; I could virtually hear it click into place as his belly laugh subsided.

He wanted to laugh again. Our game was illuminated by his brilliant new awareness. He knew we were playing a game, he knew what would happen next, he knew who I was, and he knew that I knew that he knew…. That's all it took. A tiny door opened and I could see beyond it to all the possible pleasures in store. He had stolen my heart. It was spring at last and I was in love.

Roberta Israeloff

Many people make the false assumption that because a baby can't speak he can't hear. As a result, when confronted with an infant, any infant, they raise their voices and speak very distinctly, as though they were ordering a meal in a foreign language.

Jean Kerr

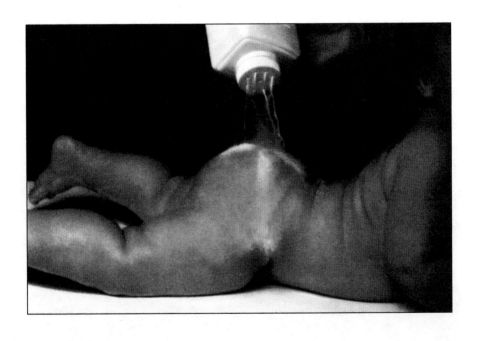

REFLECTION ON BABIES

A bit of talcum
Is always walcum.

Ogden Nash

One of the most important things to remember about infant care is: Never change diapers in midstream.

Don Marquis

You know more than you think you do.

Benjamin Spock

Getting down on all fours and imitating a rhinoceros stops babies from crying.

P. J. O'Rourke

You will always be your baby's favorite toy.

Vicki Lansky

The only thing better than a sleeping baby is a sleeping mother.

Beth Wilson Saavedra

No matter who it is that speaks, or what superlatives are employed, no baby is admired sufficiently to please the mother.

E. V. Lucas

The best thing a child can have is two parents who really love each other.

Rildia Bee Cliburn

Babies are necessary to grownups. A new baby is like the beginning of all things—wonder, hope, a dream of possibilities. In a world that is cutting down its trees to build highways, losing its earth to concrete, babies are almost the only remaining link with nature, with the natural world of living things from which we spring.

Eda J. Leshan

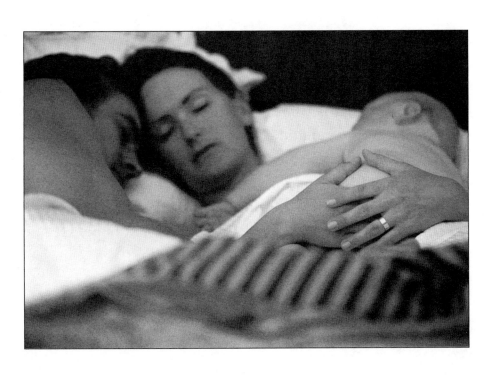

I believe that each newborn child arrives on earth with a message to deliver to mankind. Clenched in his little fist is some particle of yet unrevealed truth, some missing clue, which may solve the enigma of man's destiny. He has a limited amount of time to fulfill his mission and he will never get a second chance—nor will we. He may be our last hope. He must be treated as top sacred.

Sam Levenson

The greatness of the human personality begins at the hour of birth. From this almost mystic affirmation there comes what may seem a strange conclusion: that education must start from birth.

Maria Montessori

When you want a child, you have a lot to hope for. When you have a child, you have a lot to live for.

Jan Blaustone

If there is trouble let it be in my day, that my child may have peace.

Thomas Paine

Children are a kind of confirmation of life. The only form of immortality that we can be sure of.

Peter Ustinov

What the mother sings to the cradle goes all the way to the coffin.

Henry Ward Beecher

Train up a child in the way he should go; and when he is old, he will not depart from it.

Proverbs 22:6

A baby is God's opinion that the world should go on.

Carl Sandburg

Your children are not your children.
They are the sons and daughters of Life's longing for itself.
They come through you but are not from you,
and though they are with you, yet they belong not to you.

You may give them your love but not your thoughts,
for they have their own thoughts.
You may house their bodies but not their souls,
for their souls dwell in the house of tomorrow,
which you cannot visit, not even in your dreams.
You may strive to be like them,
but seek not to make them like you.
For life goes not backward nor tarries with yesterday.

Kahlil Gibran

Author Index

Credits

Pages 2–3: Laurie Lico Albanese for "Dancing Baby." © 1992 by Laurie Lico Albanese. The poem first appeared in the Fall 1992 issue of *Mothering*. Reprinted with the permission of the author.

Pages 45, 46: Richard Armour for "His Mother's Eyes" and "Miniature." © Geoffrey Armour. Reprinted with the permission of Kathleen S. Armour and Geoffrey S. Armour.

Page 63: The Boston Women's Health Book Collective for a quote from *The New Our Bodies, Ourselves*. © 1984, 1992 by The Boston Women's Health Book Collective. Reprinted with the permission of Simon and Schuster.

Pages 26–27: Fran Castan for "The Adoption." © 1985 by Fran Castan. Reprinted with the permission of the author.

Pages 19, 30: Barbara Crooker for "Newborn" and "Perspective." © 2001 by Barbara Crooker. Reprinted with the permission of the author.

Pages 40, 50: Susan Eisenberg for "Simon" and "The Baby." © 1987 by Susan Eisenberg. Reprinted with the permission of the author.

Page 48: Margaret Fishback for "The Anatomy of Melancholy" from *Look Who's a Mother* by Margaret Fishback. © 1945 by Margaret Fishback. Reprinted with the permission of Simon and Schuster.

Pages 58, 71: Selma Fraiberg for two quotes from *The Magic Years* by Selma Fraiberg. © 1959 by Selma Fraiberg, renewed 1987 by Louis Fraiberg and Lisa Fraiberg. Reprinted with the permission of Scribner, a division of Simon and Schuster.

Page 16: Betsy Franco for "To a Newborn." © 2001 by Betsy Franco. Reprinted with the permission of the author.

Page 85: Kahlil Gibran from *The Prophet* by Kahlil Gibran. © 1923 by Kahlil Gibran and renewed 1951 by Administrators C. T. A. of Kahlil Gibran Estate and Mary G. Gibran. Used by permission of Alfred A. Knopf, a division of Random House, Inc.

Also from Meadowbrook Press

✦ *Baby Names around the World*
Here are over 50,000 baby name choices for prospective parents with informative and interesting features including a listing of names by country of origin. So if you're looking for an Irish, Italian, Russian, African, Chinese, Japanese, or Brazilian name—or any other name from around the world—this book is for you.

✦ *The Joy of…* Series
Six treasuries of wise and warm advice for that special parent, grandparent, spouse, sister, or friend in your life. These collections reflect the wittiest and wisest (and sometimes most amusing) sentiments ever written about those whom we hold most dear. Each book is illustrated with black and white photographs that poignantly depict the unique relationships between family and friends. These books are the perfect gift to show a loved one how much you care. *The Joy of Cats, The Joy of Friendship, The Joy of Grandparenting, The Joy of Marriage, The Joy of Parenthood*, and *The Joy of Sisters*.

**We offer many more titles written to delight, inform, and entertain.
To order books with a credit card or browse our full
selection of titles, visit our web site at:**

www.meadowbrookpress.com

or call toll-free to place an order, request a free catalog, or ask a question:

1-800-338-2232

Meadowbrook Press • 5451 Smetana Drive • Minnetonka, MN • 55343